THE
LITTLE APPLE
BOOK

Mavis Budd

PIATKUS

Other titles in the series

The Little Green Avocado Book
The Little Garlic Book
The Little Pepper Book
The Little Lemon Book
The Little Strawberry Book

© 1983 Judy Piatkus (Publishers) Limited

First published in 1983 by Judy Piatkus
(Publishers) Limited of Loughton, Essex

British Library Cataloguing in Publication Data
Budd, Mavis
The little apple book.
1. Cookery (Apples)
I. Title
641.6'4'11   TX813.A6

ISBN 0–86188–253–9

Drawings by Linda Broad

Designed by Ken Leeder

Cover photograph by John Lee

Typeset by V & M Graphics Ltd, Aylesbury, Bucks
Printed and bound by The Pitman Press, Bath

CONTENTS

THE APPLE TREE

The cult of the apple flourished for centuries throughout all of Europe. There were celebrations to honour the tree; songs were sung to promote its health, and the success of its crop; offerings were made to it; its branches were doused with cider, danced under, worshipped. Whole families gathered to enjoy the revels. The apple crop was important – as it always has been and as, no doubt, it always will be.

The apple tree belongs to the genus *Malus*, a

member of the Rosaceae or Rose family, and it thrives in the temperate zones of both hemispheres. It is a hardy, deciduous tree which can grow to a height of 15 to 20 feet, or more. The leaves are ovate

and light green; the blossom, which appears in May, is rose tinted and the pretty five-petalled flowers grow in clusters. The fruit ripens in late summer and autumn, according to the variety. It is firm, good to eat, easy to handle and to store.

An apple is made up of around 50,000,000 cells, which are divided into various tissues, each with a specific function. The skin is composed of the cuticle and epidermis; several layers of cells form the hypodermis, which contains the pigments that give the fruit its characteristic green or red colour. The bulk of the flesh, known as the cortex, is filled with sap containing sugars, acids, minerals and vitamins. The core is composed of five horny carpels, each of which contains one or two seeds, or pips, surrounded by denser tissue. The core is separated from the cortex by the core line, which is joined to the stem.

Fruit appears about four to six weeks after the blossom is over, and the apple matures in about ten to 12 weeks, depending on whether it is an early or a late variety. The rapid cell division and subsequent enlargement of the cells as the apples grow, result in the fruit being very fragile; bigger apples will bruise more easily than smaller ones and will not keep as well.

There are thousands of different varieties of apples, all developed by cross-pollination and grafting from the original crab apple stock.

THE CRAB APPLE

All apples developed from the crab apple, which grows wild throughout Britain and the temperate zones of Europe and South-East Asia. There are five related species in the United States, among them the Garland Crab and the Prairie Crab. These species are regarded as native to America, but it is very possible that they were introduced from the Caucasus, where the crab is thought to have originated.

Many roadside trees, especially if the flowers are very pink, will have grown from the pips of orchard apples, discarded by passers-by or dropped by birds. Apple seeds rarely grow true, and often revert to their original stock.

The crab apple is a deciduous tree, growing to a

height of 15 to 20 feet, with dark brown bark and dense twisting branches. It grows in copses and sheltered hedgerows, and produces a mass of reddish-brown twigs and short-stalked leaves. It has beautiful pinkish-white fragrant blossom.

The fruit is small and tart, yellowish-green in colour, sometimes with large white spots, and often turning to scarlet during the late autumn. Crab apples can be picked from August to October, and are best after the mellowing and softening effect of a slight frost.

The apples are so sour that it was once the custom of the Indians in North America to gather crabs during the autumn and to bury them immediately in the ground, leaving them there until the spring. When they were dug up, they were supposed to taste far less sharp. In Britain, country people used to believe that if crabs were stored for six weeks in an old haystack they would become sweeter and more pleasant to eat!

Crab apples used to be made into 'verjuice', an acid liquor formed from sour fruit and used in cooking. And in the 16th century, they were an essential ingredient in the preparation of 'pomatum' or pomade. The word pomatum derived from 'pomum', meaning apple. The scented apple ointment was applied to the skin. Today, crab apples are used to make excellent jams, jellies and wine.

VARIETIES
OF APPLES

There are over over 2,000 varieties of apples in the world. They are divided into three main classes: dessert, cookers and cider apples. The following are the most popular varieties and the best to eat, cook and store.

POPULAR BRITISH APPLES

Cox's Orange Pippin, considered by many people to be the finest flavoured apple of all; available from late September to May. It is pale green with an orange to red flush, a firm juicy flesh and a sweet distinctive flavour.

Laxton's Superb, similar to the Cox, from which it was developed, but a little sweeter, and it ripens later.

Egremont Russet, a delicious eater, available from late September to January; it is medium-sized, with russet-brown skin tinged with orange, and a crisp nutty-flavoured flesh.

Worcester Pearmain, another delicious dessert apple, sweet and juicy with pale green streaks and reddish blush. It should be eaten as soon after picking or purchase as possible.

Similar in flavour and appearance to the Worcester Pearmain is *Tydeman's Early*, juicy, sweet-scented, but rather more round and red in colour.

Spartan, the latest of the dessert apples, has a purplish-red skin and white flesh. It keeps well.

Among the newer varieties is the *Discovery*, which is a good eater and also keeps well. It has a red skin, streaked with yellow, and a firm juicy flesh.

Crispin, another new variety which is increasing in supply; a large, greenish-yellow apple with a good flavour; available from November through to May.

COOKERS

Of the cooking apples, the *Bramley Seedling* is the best-known and is specially suitable for baking. It is large, with a waxy green skin, and is available throughout the year.

Another good cooker is the *Grenadier*; round, flattish, with a yellow-green skin; an early apple, available in August and September. *Lord Derby* is also good.

AMERICAN FAVOURITES

Among the most popular varieties in the United States is the *Winesap*, a dual-purpose apple, bright red with a firm juicy flesh, pleasantly tart. It stores, eats and cooks well.

The *Golden Delicious*, best from October to April, also rates high; it is rounded-oval in shape with a greenish-gold skin and a firm, cream-coloured flesh.

Delicious, in season from September to April, is reputed to be among the choicest eating apples in the world. It is sweet and juicy, with a broad shoulder tapering to five knob-like points around the calyx.

The *Newton* is best in March, April and May; it is a round apple with a greenish-yellow skin, perfect for eating fresh or for cooking.

The *Red Rome Beauty* is especially popular for baking.

AUSTRALIAN VARIETIES

A selection of the Australian varieties must begin with the *Granny Smith*, so called in memory of Mrs Maria Ann 'Granny' Smith, who grew the first one of its kind in 1868. Many people claim that the Granny Smith is the best apple in the world. It is an all-purpose fruit, medium-large with a green skin which changes to a buttery-yellow when ripe. It tastes delicious, cooks and keeps well. It is available for export from March to October.

Another favourite is the *Jonathan*, bright to dull red, medium-sized with white, slightly acid, flesh. It is an early main-crop apple, exported from March to May.

Red Delicious, a medium-to-large dessert apple, is very popular in Australia. Blushed with red or carmine, it has a yellowish flesh with a rich flavour, quite distinctive. Exported from March to June.

Sturmer, grown only in Tasmania, is a main-crop apple, and used chiefly for cooking. It has a greenish-yellow skin with a dull reddish blush. Exported from March to September.

Other varieties include *Democrat*, a dark red, flattish apple with a dry-sweet flesh. It keeps well and is exported from April to December. *Gravenstein*, an early apple, has a cream skin streaked with crimson, sub-acid and aromatic. *McIntosh*, another early, is crimson in colour with white flesh and a good flavour.

As time goes on, other apples will appear in the world's orchards, and many of them are bound to become family favourites in both hemispheres. The culture of trees and the development of new varieties will continue, while old favourites retain their well-earned position wherever apples are eaten.

In Britain, there is a special research centre at East Malling in Kent, where every aspect of fruit-growing is investigated by scientists; every year new varieties of apples are tested at National Fruit Trials. Research goes on in many other countries, too.

Apple-growing is big business. Standards of grading, packing and shipping are high, while storage is now so reliable that it really is possible, if we so wish, to eat an apple a day every day of the year.

APPLE GROWING REGIONS

The main apple-growing regions in Britain are in the south and south-east of England. There, the average rainfall is less than 30 inches a year, and the dryness and the summer warmth of the low hills are ideal. Also of great importance to the apple-grower is the fact that damaging late frosts and diseases caused by damp are less common in the south than in other parts of the country. Both the climate and the terrain of the north of England and Scotland are unsuitable for commercial apple growing.

The biggest growing area is Kent, with about 50% of the crop, followed by Bedfordshire and Cambridgeshire, Worcestershire and Suffolk. Homegrown apples are available in Britain throughout the year.

The main growing regions in the United States of America are Washington, Oregon and California, where the weather conditions are among the world's best for growing apples.

Washington state produces approximately one third of the American crop, and 55% of the Red Delicious variety which thrives on the long summer days and cool nights of the region.

Australia is the leading grower and exporter of apples in the Southern Hemisphere, and the fruit is grown in all six states; Tasmania is the most productive, and Western Australia is especially well-known for the production of the popular Granny Smith.

Apple-growing in Australia dates back to the arrival of the 'First Fleet' in New South Wales in 1788, and from then on the apple industry has flourished. In 1971, the country was exporting 7 million boxes of apples a year in a short shipping season which covered about 15 weeks, sending them to Britain, Europe, Singapore, Hong Kong and the USA. These exports have now declined somewhat due to increased competition. At the present time, Australia's apple production varies from 17 million to 20 million boxes a year, depending on the season, 3 million of which are exported to more than 30 countries throughout the world.

World production of apples is about 20 million tonnes a year. Europe produces about 11 million, and North America 3½ million. The USSR is a major producer but no statistics are available.

'Kent, sir – everybody knows Kent – apples, cherries, hops and women.'

Charles Dickens, *Pickwick Papers*

The world record size for an apple was achieved by one grown in Ross-on-Wye in Herefordshire, England, in 1965. It weighed 3 lbs 1 oz.

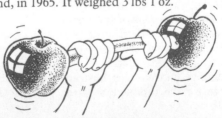

NUTRITIONAL VALUE OF APPLES

An apple is made up of 84% water, 13% sugar and acids, 0.5% minerals and vitamins, and 2.5% cellulose and pectin.

The natural sugar in apples is known as fructose. Even though the vitamins and minerals are present in small amounts, they are important to health and help convert the fructose into energy. The other constituents help to guard against disease and acid digestion.

The vitamins present in apples are mainly of the B group and include Thiamine, Riboflavin and Niacin. Vitamins A and D are present, but only a very little Vitamin C. You would need ten average-sized apples to supply the Vitamin C content found in one ripe orange. (The Cox's Orange Pippin contains slightly more Vitamin C than other varieties.)

The most abundant mineral is potassium, which works together with sodium to control body fluids, and helps the kidneys to dispose of waste substances.

The skin of the apple provides fibre, which is necessary for a healthy diet. The skin also contains a minute quantity of fat, which occurs as a waxy layer on the surface.

HISTORY OF THE APPLE

It is generally thought that the forbidden tree of the Garden of Eden was an apple tree, but the Bible does not state this specifically. In the text, the tree is referred to as 'the tree which is in the midst of the garden', and 'the woman saw that the tree *was* good for food, and that it was pleasant to the eyes, and a tree to be desired to make *one* wise, she took of the fruit thereof, and did eat, and gave also unto her husband with her; and he did eat.'

The apple tree was certainly in existence in prehistoric times. Charred remains of apples have been discovered in the mud of lake dwellings in Europe, while pips have been found embedded in pieces of ancient pottery.

The apple is mentioned in the Bible, in the Hindu

Code of Manu, in the Egyptian Book of the Dead, and in the earliest annals of China and Babylon. It featured in the writings of both Ancient Rome and Ancient Greece in the 3rd century B.C. The Roman writer Cato mentions three varieties of apple, while Homer refers to the presence of apples in the Garden of Alcinous and Laertes. Later, the Roman poet Horace writes of a banquet that lasted from 'the egg to the apple'. Even a wall of the Summer Palace of Livia, the wife of the first of the Roman Emperors, was decorated by a painting of an apple tree.

Apple trees were introduced into Britain during the Roman occupation, the first trees being planted in Somerset.

The apple became well-known to the Celts who regarded it as a symbol of rejuvination. A Welsh legend tells of a Paradise known as Avalon where Kings and heroes went after death, and which was filled with apple trees.

The earliest written record of the fruit in Britain dates back to 885. It was found in King Alfred's translation of Gregory the Great's *Pastoral Care*.

The Pearmain apple was known to have been cultivated in Norfolk during the 13th century, and in 1296 one of the first cooking apples, the 'Costard', appeared. Cider, a product of apples, followed quickly. It was certainly being drunk instead of wine during the Hundred Years War.

During the reign of Henry VIII, Pippins were brought into Britain from France. They were so called because they were grown from pips. Henry sent his chief fruiterer, Richard Harris, to France to learn about the cultivation of fruit, and especially the cultivation of the apple. He brought back to England a 'great store of graftes' and started the first apple orchard in Teynham Kent. And during the reign of Charles II, the famous cider orchards of Hertfordshire were planted.

Catharine the Great was a great apple lover. She introduced the 'Reinette d'Angleterre' into Russia from England, where it was first grown in Lord Zouch's garden at Paraham in Sussex. She even had golden pippins sent from England, each one wrapped in silver paper.

The grafting and improving of trees went on, and in 1797 Thomas Andrew Knight, a horticulturist, wrote a book entitled *Treatise on the Culture of the Apple and Pear and the manufacture of cider and perry*. Knight was especially interested in pollination experiments, and one of his disciples, Thomas Laxton, gave his name to the Laxton apples.

Early settlers took the apple to Canada, Australia and New Zealand. Captain Bligh of *Bounty* fame was responsible for introducing it to Tasmania, when a botanist from on board ship planted a tree on Brundy Island. Jan Van Riebreeck, the founder of Cape Settlement, took the apple to South Africa, and the *Mayflower* carried it to America along with the Pilgrim Fathers.

A history of the apple would not be complete without a mention of the famous apple connected with the legend of William Tell. Tell was forced by the tyrannical Austrian Viceroy, Gessler, to shoot an apple in half as it balanced on his son's head. William

Tell was a famous marksman; he accomplished the task, and later killed the evil Gessler, thus starting the 14th century Swiss War of Independence.

APPLE SUPERSTITION
AND FOLKLORE

Apples have been growing in cottage gardens for centuries, so it is no wonder that apple superstitions and customs abound. Country people were never slow to see an omen or a promise in the growing things around them, and the importance of their apple trees was certainly not overlooked.

Various customs connected with apple trees existed in different parts of Britain, and one of the most widely practised was Apple Wassailing. The word 'wassail' is derived from the Old Norse word 'vesheill' which means 'be in health', and wassailing involved numerous ceremonies and entreaties to encourage the trees to crop.

On Twelfth Night, in the West of England, the farmers and their families took pails of cider, in which they had stirred roasted apples, and went out to their orchards to toast the trees. Gathering round, with their glasses filled, they chanted:

> 'Health to thee, good apple tree
> Well to bear pocket fulls, hat fulls,
> Peck fulls, bushel fulls ...'

Then they tossed the contents of their glasses over the trees.

During Rogation week, the young men of Kent would run into the orchards and, circling each tree in turn, would sing:

> 'Stand fast root, bear well top
> God send us a youling crop
> Every twig, apple big
> Every bough, apple enow.'

In Devon, girls gathered crab apples from the hedges and arranged them to form the initials of their suitors. At dawn on Old Michaelmas Day, they inspected them. The initials in the best condition indicated the name of the man they should marry.

In Cornwall, young girls believed that they would dream of their lovers if they slept with an apple under the pillow.

In Sussex, an apple pip was placed on the bars of the grate while the following rhyme was chanted:

> 'If you love me, bounce and fly
> If you hate me, lie and die.'

Apples and Hallowe'en are inseparable. Many customs were observed, including the game of 'Apple Bobbing' which was devised, as so many customs were, as a divination of marriage.

Unmarried girls of the household used to gather round the fire, each holding an apple suspended on a string. The girl whose apple fell off first would be the first to marry.

Another custom was to peel an apple and throw the skin over the left shoulder. As it fell, it was hoped that it would form the initials of your true-love. If it broke as it fell, you would never marry.

Country people watched their apple trees for signs of what was to come.

If the sun shone through the branches of the apple tree on Christmas Day, there would be a good crop of fruit the following autumn.

People chanted:

> 'March dust on apple leaf
> Brings all kind of fruit to grief.'

It was believed that, unless the orchard was christened by a shower of rain on St Peter's Day, June 29th, the crop would be a poor one.

It was bound to be a good crop if rain fell on the trees on St Swithin's Day, July 15th.

To Test An Apple For Ripeness

To find out if an apple is ready for picking, lift it carefully in the palm of the hand as it hangs on the tree, then twist it very gently. If it is ripe, it will part easily from the branch with the stalk still attached to it. Never pull an apple from the branch, or remove the stalk.

According to country wisdom, the pips of a ripe apple will rattle if you shake it.

To Store Ripe Apples

Ripe apples should be handled carefully while they are being harvested as they bruise easily, and if bruised they will not keep.

Once picked, apples should be placed in a cool, well-ventilated place and left to sweat for a few days.

Pick out any that are damaged, diseased or do not have a stalk attached, and use them for cooking. Each apple should then be lightly wrapped in a square of newspaper, and the apples should be stored in single layers on slatted shelves. Choose a place that is dark and cool; the temperature should be about $40^0F/5^0C$.

Make sure that the apples do not touch one another. If one goes rotten, it could affect its neighbour.

Apples should never be stored with potatoes or they will lose their flavour. Nor will the potatoes taste so good or keep as well.

Apples should not be stored close to pears, either. The pears will cause the apples to over-ripen.

Country people said that if apples were to be stored, they should be gathered while the moon was sinking. Also, fruit picked and stored during the time of the full moon would not lose its plumpness.

To Dry Apples For Storing

It is a good idea to dry a few apples to make sure that you have a supply throughout the year, especially if you have no freezer.

Apple drying can be done at any time; dry them when you pick or buy them, or wait until your stored apples will not keep much longer.

DRIED APPLE RINGS

Peel and core the apples and slice into rings about ½ inch thick. The rings should not be too thin or they will shrink when dried; nor should they be too thick as they will take a long time to dry right through.

As you cut the rings, drop them into a solution of 1 oz salt to 4½ pints water, and leave them to soak for about 15 minutes. Remove from the water, place on a clean cloth and pat dry.

Arrange the rings on trays or wire racks and put in a cool oven (300°F/150°C/Gas 2) until they turn leathery. This will take about 7 hours.

Cool and store in airtight containers.

Reconstitute by soaking the dried rings in warm water.

FREEZING APPLES

Apples freeze well, but always use the best quality fruit. They may be frozen by any of four methods – sliced and blanched without sugar; puréed; partly cooked and sweetened; in a syrup pack. Apples keep in the freezer for approximately one year.

When thawing the frozen apple, remember that it will discolour on exposure to the air. Keep covered.

PREPARING APPLES

It is important to use the right apple for the right job. As a guide to which type to use for what, remember that the very acid cookers are the ones most likely to go soft and collapse. These varieties are best for making purée and apple sauce. The not-so-acid apples are best for filling pies and for baking whole.

Dessert apples retain their shape when cooked because they contain more sugar than cookers. They are ideal for making open tarts and fritters – and, in fact, any recipe that requires apple pieces to keep their shape.

Before cooking, wash, core and remove stalks, bruises and blemishes. To avoid waste, pour boiling water over the apple just before peeling it as this will make the apple peel more easily. Use a very sharp knife, or if you prefer, a potato peeler to ensure that the peel is consistently thin.

TIPS

* If prepared apples are not to be used imme-diately, place them in a bowl of salted water to prevent discolouration. Use 1 tablespoon salt to 2 pints water. lemon juice added to the water has the same effect.

* To achieve really thin slices, slice the peeled and cored apples on a cucumber, one side at a time.

* When cooking apples, avoid using saucepans made of aluminium as there is a strong chemical reaction between the acid of the apple and the metal of the pan. To see how strong this reaction is, you need only look at a stained aluminium pan after it has been used to stew apples.

* Apple preserves should be made in pans of cast iron or stainless steel.

* To prevent an apple bursting while being baked, score the skin round the middle of the apple with the tip of a very sharp knife before putting it into the oven.

* When filling a pie, always start and finish with a layer of fruit. Sugar in direct contact with pastry tends to make it sticky.

* It is a good idea to mix about 1 tablespoon cornflour with the sugar sprinkled over the fruit in an apple pie. This will thicken the juice and the pie will be easier to cut when cold.

* To finish an apple pie, brush the baked pastry lid with whisked egg-white, sprinkle with caster sugar and return to the oven for a few minutes.

* A glaze of beaten egg is much improved if a pinch of salt is added.

* Apples are delicious cooked with cloves, cinnamon, lemon, orange, quinces, rum and rosehip syrup. A spoonful of apple jelly will improve stewed apple.

* To achieve firm, crisp apple slices, toss them in a little melted butter and sprinkle them with caster sugar. Cook them very slowly in a covered dish in the oven. On no account add water.

TO STEW APPLES PERFECTLY

First, make up a syrup by heating sugar and water. The amount of sugar depends on the tartness of the apples, but 4 oz sugar to 1 lb fruit with ½ pint water is about right.

Core, peel and slice the apples into ¼ inch rings, or quarter and then slice them. When the sugar has dissolved in the warm water, add the apples, cover and cook very gently for 10-15 minutes until just tender. Do not boil or the fruit will collapse into pulp.

Drain the apples carefully, reserving the syrup, and place the stewed apples in a warm serving dish. Boil the syrup very fast until it thickens, and pour over the fruit.

A GUIDE TO COOKING TIMES

* Quartered apple segments need to cook for about 10-15 minutes.
* Dried apple rings need to cook for about 30 minutes.
* Baked apples take 30-45 minutes, rather more or less according to the type and size of apple.

SOUP

APPLE SOUP

This is a refreshingly tart soup; the recipe comes from Pennsylvania.

2 lbs firm apples
4 pints water
¼ teaspoon cinnamon
4 oz sugar
juice of ½ lemon
grated rind of 1 lemon
2 tablespoons cornflour
2 oz redcurrants, cleaned
1 glass red or white wine
salt

Core the apples and slice them thinly without peeling them. Stew them in the water with the cinnamon, sugar, lemon juice and grated rind until the apples are soft. Mix the cornflour with a little cold water until it has the consistency of thin cream, then stir it into the soup and let it bubble for a few minutes.

Add the redcurrants and the wine and season with salt only. Bring the soup back to the boil and simmer slowly for about 7 minutes. Strain through a fine sieve, then cool and chill in the refrigerator. Serve ice cold.

Serves 6

SAVOURY DISHES

APPLE AND SHRIMP SALAD

This makes an unusual and rather exotic salad.

For the dressing:
1 tablespoon lemon juice
coffee cupful good mayonnaise

For the salad:
½ small green pepper
1 large cooking apple, peeled and thinly sliced
2 sticks celery
4 oz shrimps, halved
1 small lettuce
stuffed olives, to garnish

Mix together the lemon juice and the mayonnaise.
   Pour boiling water over the pepper, dry carefully
and remove the seeds and the ribs, then slice very
thinly. Chop the apple and celery into fairly small
pieces and mix with the pepper. Add the halved
shrimps, pour the dressing over the salad and mix
thoroughly.
   Heap the salad on a bed of crisp lettuce leaves and
garnish with stuffed olives.

Serves 4

APPLE AND CELERY COLESLAW

Apples make a delicious addition to coleslaw, which goes well with cold meats and poultry.

½ small white cabbage
2 dessert apples
3 sticks celery, chopped small
3 tablespoons olive oil
1 tablespoon vinegar
2 tablespoons mayonnaise
salt and pepper

Wash the cabbage and remove any damaged leaves, then shred finely. Place in a large bowl, then grate the apples and add to the cabbage together with the chopped celery. Add all the other ingredients and mix well. Allow the coleslaw to stand for a short time before serving.

Serves 4

SANDWICH FILLINGS

1. Chop a few dates and an apple, mix together and bind with mayonnaise. Sandwich between slices of thin brown bread and butter.

2. To make a sandwich spread, grate 2 medium dessert apples, chop 4 small pickled beetroot, and combine with a little juice from the beets, 4 tablespoons mayonnaise and salt and pepper to taste. Chill before using.

3. For an open sandwich, use grated cheese and apple with a scant sprinkling of paprika pepper.

4. Colour cream cheese with a dash of paprika and add a little celery, finely chopped. Spread on brown bread and decorate with slices of red-skinned apple.

PORK FILLET WITH APPLE

Apples go extremely well with rich meat and poultry, such as pork and goose. The tartness of the apples helps to neutralise the richness of the meat. Apple sauce with pork is well-known to everyone, but here is a recipe which is a little different.

1 pork fillet
2 oz butter and oil
salt and pepper
1 large cooking apple
1 oz caster sugar

Beat the pork fillet flat with a wooden kitchen mallet or the back of a large wooden spoon until it is quite thin.

Heat the butter and oil in a heavy frying pan and fry the fillet gently on both sides until tender. If the meat is really thin, this will take about 15 minutes. Drain, season with salt and pepper and keep hot.

Peel and core the apple and cut into rings about ½ inch thick. Lightly fry on both sides in the fat in the pan. Sprinkle with the sugar and continue frying until the sugar melts.

Serve the apple rings with the meat.

Serves 2 – 3

STUFFING FOR GOOSE

Apples soaked in rum make a delicious stuffing for a goose.

To stuff a 10 lb bird:
6 good-sized cooking apples
2-4 tablespoons rum
½ teaspoon finely chopped sage
½ teaspoon ground mace
12 oz coarse breadcrumbs
salt and black pepper
stock or apple juice

Peel and core the apples and chop them into small pieces. Soak them in the rum for 4 to 5 hours, then add the sage, ground mace and breadcrumbs and season to taste with salt and pepper.

Mix all the ingredients together and add a little stock or apple juice if you find the consistency too dry. Stuff the goose just before roasting.

Deer are extremely partial to crab apples; it is said that many trees were planted by ecclesiastics who were extremely fond of a plump hart for dinner ...

APPLE PUDDINGS
APPLE AND CHEESE PANCAKES

These are delicious topped with a little sour cream.

Batter:
4 oz plain flour
pinch of salt
1 egg
½ pint of milk
oil for frying

Filling:
8 oz cream cheese
4 oz raisins
1 medium dessert apple, peeled, cored and chopped
grated rind of 1 lemon
caster sugar, to serve

Sift the flour and salt into a large bowl. Beat the egg with the milk and stir gradually into the flour. Mix until smooth. Heat a very little oil in a frying pan, pour 2 tablespoons batter into the centre of the pan and tilt to spread the batter. Cook for 1 minute on each side. Make all the pancakes and keep warm.

Meanwhile mix the filling ingredients together very well. Fill the pancakes with spoonfuls of the filling, then roll up and dust with caster sugar.

Makes 8-10 pancakes

APPLE FRITTERS

An ideal way to use up a glut of cooking apples.

3 large cooking apples, peeled, cored and cut into
  ¼ inch slices
4 tablespoons cider
2 tablespoons sugar

Batter:
4 oz plain flour
1 teaspoon baking powder
good pinch salt
1 oz butter, melted
1 tablespoon cider
¼ pint milk
white of 1 egg, stiffly beaten
oil for deep frying
icing sugar, to serve

Arrange the apple slices in a shallow dish. Mix together the cider and sugar and pour over the apples. Allow to soak for at least 1 hour.

Make the batter by sifting the flour, baking powder and salt into a bowl. Stir in the melted butter and cider. Beat in the milk, a little at a time until the mixture is smooth. Fold in the egg white.

Dip the apple pieces in the batter and allow the excess to drip off. Deep fry several apple slices at a time in hot oil until golden brown. Drain on kitchen paper and keep hot. Serve sprinkled with icing sugar.

Serves 4-6

ENGLISH APPLE PIE

A traditional apple pie, to be served warm or cold, with cream or cheese.

8 oz shortcrust pastry
2 lbs cooking apples
4 oz sugar
juice of ½ lemon
4 cloves
milk, to glaze
icing sugar, to serve

Make the pastry and leave to chill for 30 minutes. Heat the oven to 425°F/220°C/Gas 7.

Peel, core and quarter the apples and drop them into bowl of water to which a little lemon juice has been added.

Roll out two-thirds of the pastry and line a shallow 7 inch pie dish. Cut the apple pieces in half and place in layers on the pastry. Sprinkle the layers with sugar and lemon juice, and distribute the cloves. The top layer of apple pieces should be slightly domed.

Roll out remaining pastry and cover the pie, sealing the edges with a little water. Press firmly all round and make a decorative edging. Brush the top with milk and sugar. Bake for 20 minutes, then reduce the heat to 350°F/180°C/Gas 4 and continue to cook for 15-20 minutes until the top is brown.

Sprinkle with icing sugar before serving.

Serves 4-6

APPLE AND MINCEMEAT CHARLOTTE

No one seems to know exactly how Apple Charlotte originated, or why it was so called, but everyone will surely agree that it is a delicious pudding and a great children's favourite. The following recipe is a variation on a familiar theme, and very tasty.

brown or wholemeal bread, buttered
mincemeat
1 lb cooking apples, peeled, cored and sliced
2 oz brown sugar

Grease a 1 pint ovenproof dish and line it with thin slices of buttered bread. Spread a layer of mincemeat (as much or as little as you like) on the bread. Add a layer of sliced apples.

Repeat the mincemeat and apple layers.

Sprinkle the top layer of apples with most of the sugar, and cover with more thin slices of buttered bread, butter side up. Sprinkle a little more sugar over the top. Bake at 425°F/210°C/Gas 7 for about 30 minutes.

Serve hot with cream.

Serves 4

APPLE AMBER

For a special occasion the meringue can be decorated
with glacé cherries before putting into the oven.

6 oz shortcrust pastry
1 lb cooking apples
3 tablespoons water
2 oz sugar
juice and finely grated rind of ½ lemon
2 eggs, separated
3 oz caster sugar

Preheat the oven to 380°F/190°C/Gas 5.

Roll out the pastry and line an 8 inch flan tin. Bake
blind for 12-15 minutes, then lower the heat to
300°F/150°C/Gas 2.

Meanwhile core, wash and chop the apples (there is
no need to peel them), and stew them with the water
for 10 minutes until soft. Sieve them to make a purée,
then add the 2 oz sugar (or more if you prefer), the
lemon juice and rind. Beat the egg yolks and add to the
apple mixture. Pour into the flan case.

Whisk the egg whites until stiff, then add the caster
sugar, a little at a time. Cover the apple mixture with
the meringue and bake in a cool oven for 30 minutes
until the top is lightly browned.

Serve hot or cold with cream.

Serves 4

APPLE SNOW

A very easy pudding, served very cold with either cream or a wine sauce.

1½ lb cooking apples
3 tablespoons water
4 oz vanilla sugar
juice of 1 lemon
3 egg whites, beaten very stiff

Chop the apples whole (there is no need to peel and core), and stew them in the water until tender. Strain through a sieve to make a purée. Add the sugar and lemon juice. Set the purée aside until cold.

When cold, fold in the beaten egg whites, and whisk the mixture until it becomes thick.

Refrigerate and serve very cold.

Serves 4-6

WINE SAUCE

½ pint white wine or cider
4 oz caster sugar
3 egg whites

Whisk all the ingredients together over hot water until thick.

Serve very hot.

APPLE CARAMEL

An elegant and easy dish for a dinner party.

4 large apples
2 oz caster sugar
¼ pint whipping cream
3 oz soft brown sugar

Peel, core and slice the apples and poach them in a little water with the caster sugar for a few minutes so that they are still firm. Place the slices in a fireproof dish and add a few tablespoons of the poaching liquid.

Whip the cream, spread on top of the apples, and refrigerate. When the cream is well chilled, sprinkle with the soft brown sugar and place under a hot grill until the sugar starts to bubble. Remove from the heat, cool and refrigerate again for about 15 minutes.

Serves 4

At an entertainment given by Sir Watkin William Wynn, Bart, in April 1770 to celebrate his coming of age, 108 apple pies were provided among the refreshments to feed his 15,000 guests.

VERY EASY APPLE CREAM

Children love this.

4 dessert apples
2 oz caster sugar
¼ pint condensed milk

Peel, core and grate the apples. Add the sugar to the condensed milk and combine with the grated apple. Mix well and heap into a glass dish.

Serve very cold.

Serves 4-5

BAKED APPLES

Baked apples are good to eat, easy to prepare and have been on family menus for generations. The variations for the fillings are endless – a creative cook can think up dozens of ideas to ring the changes and turn an ordinary dish into something quite fantastic.

Basic preparation:
Wash and core the apples, allowing 1 per person.

Score a thin line round the middle of each apple with the point of a very sharp knife.

Stand the apples in a buttered dish and fill the centres with whichever stuffing you choose.

Bake in a moderate oven (180°F/350°C/Gas 4) for about 45 minutes, until the apples are soft and the outer skins are nicely browned. Basting the apples with a little butter as they cook improves the look of the apples and the flavour.

Suggested fillings:
1. Chopped nuts and raisins, with a small knob of butter placed on top.
2. Mashed bananas.
3. Dried apricots, soaked first in water overnight, mashed and mixed with a little honey.
4. Chopped dates mixed with grated nuts and a little lemon juice.
5. A mixture made up of 4 tablespoons each of ground almonds and brown sugar and 2 tablespoons of water.
6. A teaspoon of apple jelly added to the fillings can also be very tasty.

APPLE STRUDEL

You can buy sheets of Apple Strudel pastry in many delicatessens.

8 oz ready-made strudel dough
1½ lbs cooking apples
2 oz each currants and stoned raisins
2 oz dry breadcrumbs, fried gently in 1 oz butter
4 oz caster sugar
½ teaspoon ground cinnamon
grated peel of ½ lemon
4 oz butter, melted
icing sugar, to serve

Following the manufacturer's instructions, unfold the strudel dough and lay it carefully on a clean floured teacloth.

Peel, core and slice the apples very thinly and mix with the remaining ingredients except the butter.

Brush the strudel dough with half the melted butter and spread the filling on, leaving a ½ inch border except for the edge nearest to you. Pick up the two nearest corners of the cloth and gently roll up the strudel away from you. Pinch the edges firmly together and place on a well-buttered baking sheet, making a horseshoe shape if necessary.

Brush well with the remaining melted butter and bake at 425°F/210°C/Gas 7 for 20 minutes, then lower the temperature to 350°F/180°C/Gas 4 and cook for a further 20 minutes until the sides are crisp.

Serve hot or cold sprinkled with icing sugar.

Serves 6

APPLE CAKE
APPLE HONEY SPONGE

This sponge is lovely served with whipped cream for afternoon tea.

2 lbs cooking apples
4 tablespoons honey
2 tablespoons water
4 oz butter, softened
2 oz caster sugar
2 eggs, beaten
milk, to moisten
8 oz self-raising flour, sifted
pinch of salt

Peel, core and slice the apples and stew them gently with half the honey and 2 tablespoons water to stop it sticking. Pour the purée into a buttered pie dish.

Beat the butter, sugar and the remaining honey to a cream and add the eggs, a little at a time. If the mixture seems dry, add a little milk to moisten, then stir in the sifted flour and salt.

Cover the apples with the sponge mixture and bake at 350°F/180°C/Gas 4 for 30 minutes.

APPLE SAUCES
RAW APPLE SAUCE

This sauce can be frozen very successfully.

¾ cup apple juice
2 cups apple pieces
½ cup raisins
pinch cinnamon
honey, to sweeten

Put the apple juice in a blender, add the apples and reduce to a pulp.

Stir in raisins, cinnamon and honey to taste.

Serves 4-6

APPLE SAUCE WITH ORANGE AND PICKLE

This sauce is good with cold meats and poultry.

½ pint thick apple purée
2 tablespoons sweet pickle
1 tablespoon malt vinegar
2 tablespoons orange marmalade
salt and pepper

Heat the purée and stir in the pickle, the vinegar and marmalade. Add a little salt and pepper to taste and serve at once.

Serves 4

PRESERVES
APPLE BUTTER

An old-fashioned preserve, lovely at tea time.

6 lbs apples (cooking, or crab)
2 pints water
2 pints cider
1 teaspoon ground cloves
1 teaspoon ground cinnamon
1 teaspoon ground nutmeg
1 lb sugar (either granulated or soft brown, or a
   mixture of the two) to 1 pint pulp

Cut the apples into pieces (there is no need to peel them), and simmer gently in the water and cider until soft. Put the pulp through a sieve and weigh, then continue to simmer it until it is thick. Stir the sugar and spices into the pulp, and continue to cook until mixture is quite firm and there is no liquid left.

Pour into hot sterilised jars and cover.

Makes about 8 lbs

APPLE-GINGER JAM

A delicately flavoured aromatic jam.

3 lbs cooking apples
1 pint water
1 teaspoon ground ginger
grated rind and juice of 2 good-sized lemons
3 lbs preserving sugar
4 oz crystalised ginger

Peel, core and cut up the apples. Put the peel, core and pips into a muslin bag and place in the pan along with the apples, water, ground ginger, and the grated rind and juice of the lemons. Simmer until the fruit is tender.

Remove the muslin bag and squeeze gently to extract all the juice. Add the sugar and the crystalised ginger, finely chopped. Stir until the sugar is dissolved, then boil fast until setting point is reached – about 15 minutes.

Pour into hot sterilised jars and cover.

Makes 5 lbs

APPLE PICKLE

This pickle can be used in a week to 10 days if required.

1 lb small sharp apples or crab apples
1 lb onions
2 oz sultanas
1 oz raisins
6-8 peppercorns
1½ oz chillies
8 cloves
1 pint vinegar
1 tablespoon sea salt

Peel, core and chop the apples, plunge them into bowl of boiling water and leave for about 3 minutes, then remove and strain carefully.

Peel and chop the onions.

Pack the apple pieces, onions, sultanas and raisins into hot jars. Tie the peppercorns, chillies and cloves in a piece of muslin. Pour the vinegar into a pan and add the bag of spices and the salt and leave to steep for 30 minutes.

Bring the vinegar to the boil, simmer for 10-15 minutes, then remove the spices. Pour this boiling vinegar over the apples and cover securely.

Makes about 4 lbs

APPLE CHUTNEY

Very good with cold meat and cheeses.

2 lbs apples
2 lbs green tomatoes
1 lb onions
1 lb sugar
2 pints vinegar
½ oz chillies
1 lb raisins
2 tablespoons coarse salt

Peel, core and chop up the apples, cut the tomatoes into chunks and peel and chop the onions. Place in a large pan with the rest of the ingredients and bring to the boil, stirring until the sugar has dissolved. Simmer until nicely browned, thick and smooth – about 1½ hours.

Pour into hot sterilised jars and cover.

Makes about 4 lbs

TWO APPLE DRINKS

APPLE ALE

A spicy drink ideal for a teenage party.

2 lbs windfall apples
1 gallon water
1½ lbs white sugar
½ teaspoon cloves
½ teaspoon cinnamon
1 oz root ginger, well bruised

Wash the apples and grate them (without peeling or coring) into a jug. Add the cold water and cover with a thick cloth. Leave to stand in a warm room for 1 week, stirring the liquor each day.

At the end of the week strain and add the sugar, cloves and cinnamon and the ginger. Stir well and leave to stand overnight.

Finally, strain into sterilised bottles and cork tightly. The ale is ready to drink in about a week.

In 1665 or 1666, Sir Isaac Newton discovered the law of gravitation when he watched an apple fall from a tree.

APPLE TODDY

Children will love this toddy.

2 large cooking apples
1 pint water
1 tablespoon honey
½ teaspoon bicarbonate of soda

Wash the apples and cut into pieces, including the peel and cores. Place in a deep pan, add the water and cover with a lid. Simmer slowly until the apples are soft, then press through a sieve.

Add the honey and the bicarbonate of soda, which will make the drink 'fizz'.

Sip while hot.

APPLES
FOR SLIMMERS

An average-size apple contains about 70 calories and is a great stand-by for slimmers. Eating an apple an hour before a meal is one way to help you eat less during the meal. The apple supplies the bulk, which not only reduces the pangs of hunger and the risk of eating too much, but will nourish you as well. And there are dozens of delicious low-calorie apple recipes.

* A baked apple, even without sugar, can be tasty, especially if you choose one of the less tart varieties. If you really can't take it without a sweetener, mix together a teaspoon of lemon juice and a teaspoon of clear honey and trickle it over the fruit.

* For a slimming open sandwich, moisten a raw apple in lemon juice, add finely chopped celery, mix with cottage cheese and eat with a piece of crispbread.

* Make a quick nutritious salad: chop up a dessert apple, mix it with watercress and dress with lemon juice.

* Or try an apple and cheese savoury. Peel, core and slice 4 dessert apples. Place them in a shallow, heat-proof dish, sprinkle with 1 oz grated Cheddar cheese, and put under a hot grill until the cheese melts. Eat while still hot. (Enough for two.)

* Apple and carrot salad is just as good. Grate 4 carrots, chop 4 dessert apples, and rinse them in lemon water. Add 1 oz raisins, and pile the mixture on to lettuce leaves and trickle over a dressing of lemon juice mixed with a little honey.

* A nourishing drink can be made by putting 2 whole apples through a juicer.

* There's a splendid apple juice which is thought to be especially good during a temporary reduction in food consumption; it helps to burn up unwanted fat while neutralising the effects of uric acid, which it also helps to expel. The juice should be sipped very slowly, otherwise much of its valuable effect will be lost.

   Mix together ½ cup of fresh apple juice, ½ cup of fresh orange juice, 2 teaspoons of lemon juice and 1 level teaspoon of clear honey.

* A delicious julep for slimmers can be made with 4 cups of apple juice, 2 cups of pineapple juice and 1 cup of fresh orange juice. Pour all the ingredients into a jug and chill. Just before serving, add slivers of lemon and sprigs of mint.

Make some of the following salad combinations:
1. Chopped apple, celery, grated cheese and freshly chopped mint.

2. Chopped apple and celery, a few slices of banana, all mixed with a dressing of natural yoghurt.

3. Apple, celery and watercress with cottage cheese.

4. Red cabbage, finely shredded, and mixed with chunks of unpeeled apples.

5. Slices of apples, a few slices of bananas, and cherries, mixed together and dressed with oil and lemon.

6. Chopped apple, shredded white cabbage and a few olives, served in a nest of crisp lettuce leaves and dressed with lemon and a very little olive oil.

APPLES AND HEALTH

T he saying that 'an apple a day keeps the doctor away' is anything but the superstitious advice of tongue-wagging old wives, though they do have many strange practices to recommend.

The apple contains valuable acids which neutralise with certain acids present in the body, leaving an alkaline deposit. Thus, the pulp of a freshly-grated apple is considered to be good for treating intestinal infections as it supplies soft bulk which helps to restore normal intestinal function. The idea that to eat an apple before going to bed helps to combat

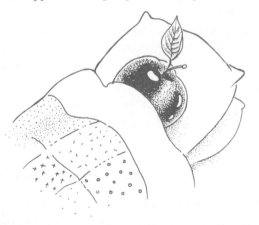

insomnia is no myth either, for the acid in the apple helps to soothe the stomach and allay any mild indigestion that could otherwise disturb one's rest.

Biting into the firm, juicy flesh of an apple can also help to clean the teeth, removing deposits of sugar and starchy food that could start decay and set up infection in the gums. If you are unable to brush your teeth before going to bed, eating an apple is certainly the next best thing you can do.

Museli
Chopped apple added to museli makes a healthy and well-balanced meal.

1 tablespoon rolled oats
1 teaspoon lemon juice
1 large unpeeled dessert apple, chopped
a few chopped nuts
yoghurt thinned with a little milk

Mix all the ingredients together, and trickle over a little honey. Eat at breakfast.

Pectin, which is found in apples, is thought to reduce the cholesterol levels in the body. It is believed by some people that for every 1 lb of apples eaten, the cholesterol level can be reduced by 1%.

The old wives had numerous things to say about apples ... They believed that a hot poultice prepared from rotten apples and applied to the painful area would relieve the sufferer of rheumatism. They also believed that a poultice of apples could soothe strained eyes.

To make the old wives' soothing poultice, you need two large cooking apples and two tablespoons of water. Cut up the apples and cook in the water until soft, then mash them until very smooth. Spread the purée on a clean cloth (a fine handkerchief was considered ideal). Fold the cloth over and place the poultice on the eyes for 15 minutes. Not only should the eyes be soothed, but the relaxation should restore the whole body.

John Pechy, a one-time member of the College of Physicians in London, said in his book about herbal remedies that the apple could cure melancholy. This book, *The Compleat Herbal of Physical Plants* included the following recipe:

The Altering Syrup of Apples
Take the juice of fragrant pippins, two Quarts of the Leaves of Garden and Wild Buglofs, of the Flowers of Violets each one Pound: boyle them in B.M. and clarafie them: add feven pounds of fine sugar, and a Pint of Rofe-water: boyle them to a Syrup. One Ounce of this Syrup, taken Morning and Evening is good for melancholy People.

It was once believed that if you ate an apple at midnight on Hallowe'en you would not get a cold for a year.

BEAUTY HINTS

As a beauty treatment, the great value of the apple lies in the good it does you by eating it, especially if you eat it whole, uncooked and unpeeled – core and pips as well. Thus all the goodness contained in it is utilised.

However, there are external beauty treatments to be made from apples, including a soothing face pack which will not only leave the skin feeling refreshed but will help to firm the tissues and combat wrinkles.

To make the face pack, cook a large apple to a pulp and, when cool, mash it and spread it over the face. A spoonful of clear honey can be beaten into the pulp to enrich it.

* In the 16th century, pomatum (apple pulp mixed with rosemary) was sold as a beauty cream.

* In Ancient Rome, apple pulp was mixed with lanolin, the grease from sheep's wool, to make a beauty cream.

* The old wives believed that an apple could cure a wart. The apple was cut in half and the two inner sides rubbed on the wart. The apple was then buried in the garden and as the pieces rotted, so the wart disappeared.

* To remove stains from the fingers after preparing apples, rub them with the inner side of the peel before washing the hands.

GROWING AN APPLE TREE FROM A PIP

The best and most reliable way to acquire an apple tree, if you want to grow your own fruit, is to buy one from a reputable nursery, where they will be able to tell you the name of the root stock. There's no reason why you should not grow one from a pip if you wish to – as long as you do not expect the tree you raise from the seed of some specially delicious apple to produce a crop of similarly delicious apples. Apples do not produce true from seed, though it is a fact that many well-known varieties originated from chance seedlings. The famous Golden Delicious originated from a chance seedling discovered in West Virginia in 1890. The Australian apple, Democrat, began as a chance seedling, too – it was discovered in an orchard in Glenorchy, Tasmania, sometime around 1900.

Apples which have been kept all winter yield the best pips for planting. Sow them in early spring, after soaking them for a few hours in tepid water. Fill 3 inch pots with good soil and plant the pips ½ inch deep. Cover the pots with a plastic bag to keep the soil damp, but remove as soon as little shoots appear.

Once a little shoot has appeared, which will be in about 1 to 2 months, maybe less in warm conditions, take care not to let the soil dry out or the seedling will die. Do not over-water, either, or it will rot off.

When the seedling has grown to about 6 inches, it can be transferred to a larger pot, and later planted out in the garden. In due course it will bear fruit, and whatever the tree might turn out to be, the fruit will certainly have its uses, for even the smallest tart apples are good for pickles and preserves.

PLANTING AN APPLE TREE

If you decide to grow an apple tree in your garden, the greatest danger to it will be a late spring frost. If the tree is in full bloom at the time, not only will the blossom die, but your hope of a bumper crop of apples too.

Commercial growers have scientifically-controlled methods for coping with the damaging effects of frost, which unfortunately are not available to the amateur fruit grower. The only thing you can do is to plant your tree in a position where it is most likely to escape the danger of frost, and also to protect it from strong winds which can cause almost as much havoc.

Choose a sheltered place where your tree will be protected and will get all the sunlight and warmth it needs. Plant it during the spring or autumn in well-drained, well-aerated, slightly alkaline soil. The roots must be able to develop and spread if the tree is to grow healthily, so take care not to pack the soil too tightly. Stake the tree carefully so that there can be no risk of the wind loosening it before it is established. On no account allow the soil to dry out, especially during the growing season, or your tree will die.

Watch out for disease, and pests such as scab (black spots on leaves and fruit), mildew (a white furry mould on leaves and shoots), and canker (rough lesions on woody shoots and branches). Deal with these promptly, but check that the remedy you select is of no danger to the environment. Manufacturers now make sprays that ensure that pests and diseases can be dealt with without fear. To use a product that would kill the bees that pollinate the blossom would do as much harm as, and probably a good deal more than, a frost.

Your apple tree will need to be pruned and it is essential that this is done correctly, not only to shape the tree but to encourage growth in the right places so it will bear well. During the first few years, scaffold branches must be distributed along the trunk and there must be no weak crotches that could crack either under the weight of fruit or in a high wind.

With your tree well-established, you might like to follow an old custom ... and plant nasturtiums beneath it. This was once thought to prevent an attack of white fly.

And you should remember the old saying: 'You don't make an apple ... it grows.'

ACKNOWLEDGEMENTS

The Apple and Pear Development Council

Department of Trade and Resources in conjunction with the Department of Primary Industry, and the Australian Apple and Pear Corporation

Washington State Apple Commission

My thanks are also due to my sister Jone Budd who helped me in my researches and in checking facts.

And to everyone who has given me recipes ...